THANK YOU

To Judy, for being faster than the average grandma

To Derek, for inspiring me to write about jeggings, among other things

To Matthew John, for being free spirited, even on a cloudy day

To John F. McGee, for coining the phrase, "Oh, that'll do"

And to my readers, though they are few and far between.

YOU'RE CONTRIBUTIONS ARE GREATLY APPRECIATED

Table of Contents

"Clouds came floating into my life, No longer to carry rain or usher a storm, but to add color to my sunset sky"

—Rabindranath Tagore

Create

Creativity:
A vast, smeared harmony
Growing in the hyacinth

Life Sways
Like a soft rose in my grip

The rose is at peace
In the forest, a black heaven

A distant school of rain
tortures butterflies
But even more distant butterflies
are the teachers

Slippery flippers imagine
Pursuing silver misery
Now
the flippers imagine leaping
from quiet mountains.

It is all Creation

Ink Run

My pen
moves across the page
like a zebra bounding across the plains.
Its hooves pound the paper
faster and faster
and faster
to escape that great predator
which is the deadline.
Unsure footing causes it to lose
control, treading softly over words
not commonly used in speech.
It pauses for a moment,
scratches behind my ear, believing
in the safety of good writing.
In an instant
it feels hot breath on its neck
and the fatal roar,
"Let's wrap it up now, finish your
sentence. Any volunteers to share?"
My pen
is nailed down now,
longing
for one more chance,
run a little faster next time.

The Velociraptor

The Velociraptor bites
your evolutionary mind
with fear of what
goes bump in the night.
But the Velociraptor
doesn't go bump,
it is silent
until it goes rip,
and then tear,
and then kill.
Clever enough
to open the mail
and carrying the equipment, too.
But although the mere thought of it
may cause you
to quiver with fear
You're alone
in the dark
The Velociraptor
is no longer here.

Forgetfulness
When I first saw you
I had high hopes
and delicious dreams.

You were my popcorn in
the microwave, my top ramen
on the stove.

I should not have left you,
that's for sure,
but life isn't always
what it seems.

While I busied myself
with ambition and efficiency
I left you all alone.

Removing my ear buds,
I hear you popping.
Walking into the kitchen,
I smell your smoke.

Oh, I wish I didn't
have to remember you
now.

Forgive Me

I'm sorry that
I told you to
suck it up and
bite the bullet

Your emotions
were a maelstrom;
They were blocking
Logic's radar.

A sinking boat,
you brought us down
and clearly I
was in the right

Like a burner
on bare skin, your
flash was badly
singed. Sorry,

Don't touch the stove
next time.
Forgive me.

55 Fiction

A collection of fictional events described each in exactly 55 words.

Gloves

My world was swimming from the impact of what he'd done. My gaze returned to his, my knees weak, and I could see his passion burning. I threw my arms around his neck; I could scarcely stand without him. Then he punched me again, I hit the canvas hard, and the ref counted to 10.

Let us Not Mince Words

My Focus is intense -- adding the final touches, the most crucial point in a writing piece. My fiction is elegantly written, witty, and exactly 55 words long. Each, I have painstakingly positioned. No fillers, no contractions. Wrapping up the final line... just to be safe, I better check the word count. 56? Son of a

Insecurities

My fingers run through thick dark hair,
down his chest and back, grasping;
feeling every inch. I point to his coat,
and he removes it. He's getting frisky.
Fingertips experienced, knowing every
curve, crevice. He's nervous. I discover
with surprise the firm bulk pressing
through his underwear. "Son, I'm
afraid you're not boarding that plane."

The N-Word

"Your word will be, 'Negus'"
"Umm, excuse me, what?"
"Negus."
"Could you us it in a sentence please?"
"In the 19th century, Negus ruled much
of Africa."
"Ahem. Negus... definition, please?"
"Negus—Family of rulers in Ethiopia,
circa 1880."
"Ahem. Negus –N—E—G—U—S—
Negus"
*ding! "You are correct."

Haiku

A collection of three-line poems using 5 syllables, 7 Syllables, 5 syllables.

Tea sits quietly;
Smoldering dark liquid peace
just an aroma

Darkness smells brand new
Pitter Patter on windows;
but I am asleep

Screams echo from hearts
Through the fingers into strings;
And the purple haze

Brothers cry at night
We all try to hide the tears;
Toe tag Jamie Smith

Eyebrows blown back flat
Beats ripple windows, fluid;
D-d-drop the bass

Detention ladies
Talk about the strangest things;
Ear buds not allowed

Eighty Eight keys wide;
Each one unlocks something new
Open the soul's doors

Mr. Kelly's beard;
Spunky patch of bear's belly
Free spirit face cloud

Red in the morning
Pink purple mounds of low sky;
No need for sailing

Coffee Flavored skin
Smooth voiced God of young wild girls;
Bruno Mars, my hero

ABC

Actions Beyond Character

Does everyone feel good
having innate justice,
knowing liability meets nullification?

Or perhaps
quiet revenge
soothes the voracious warmonger.

X-ray your zealotry.

This turtle is a pair of jeggings

This turtle is a pair of jeggings
Caught between safety and freedom,
He lives a life of uncertainty
A motion catches the corner
of his little orange eye
Then he smells the predator
on a shifting wind
Tasting the salt in the air
Then the world rattles shut
like a rickety gate
and a soft thump resounds through
the darkness
Even as he smells the shrieks,
the twigs snapping,
the air raid sirens wailing,
From inside his shell he longs to see
and feel them.

He was an egg in the beginning
When he kicked off
his existence
"Wow! that actually did make sense!"
He says,
but really it didn't,
he's just pretending.

He has to make the weighty decisions
because a turtle's mind is always full
of scales

Meanwhile jeggings,
like a sopping wet summer day,
lie in question of their own existence
Caught in befuddlement somewhere
between a liberal Bill O'Reilly and a
New York City full of Canadians,
they live a life
in the worst
of both worlds.
"Ichiban sukida yo" J.B. says,
"my favorite!"
It isn't his favorite,
he doesn't even think it is,
but evolution
often favors the
unnecessary.

And so the jeggings, like this turtle, are
trapped between
egg and adult, soft and hard, reality
and facade.

There always will be these
would be champions,
too timid to excel

And there will always be rock lizards
which are not actually made out of
rocks.

But supposing the turtle
were to wear the jeggings...
Then perhaps he would realize
that pretending is for chumps,
not reptiles.
But his mind still
is full of scales;
Soft and hard, inside and outside, the
egg and adulthood,
stretchy pants.

Dinosaurs

Local Dinosaurs
Gone but not forgotten
Wild things
Uncovering secrets of the
The loneliest
Around
A life
Has history
Gold
Survey says…
In America
Games can be WON WITHOUT
BONES TO PICK

Oh, that'll do
Eyes swelter helter skelter
Glances fleeting sheep are bleating

Share with me, I believe you're love
Carry me, retreating like a blue dove in spring

All I see is your failing health
And the pony is a neighing shelf—
to put my ambition on and wait for you

Shatter and scatter the pieces of me
you always have been one
Floating away to where I cannot go
Behind the sun

Rest in peace
My inspiration
Rest in peace
Father of father of mine

Raising hell-bent grape freeze house
dirt in the shop waits for you to return

I can barely see, I fear the darkness
You can share the glee, clearness,
sharpness

An angel is your grandson now
Its strange that you will teach him
how--to be dirty and wet, but loving
you

Shatter and scatter the pieces of me
you always have been around
Seems to me that the skies are all clear
You're clear cutting them now

Rest in peace
I love
you
rest in peace
Father of father of mine.

The Grizzly Tree

There was a tree in the forest, just where one might suspect a tree to be. It was a small tree, its roots stretching down no further than an elephant's trunk and its branches still scraping for rays of sun. It was not the sort of tree which one might think all that special, but one's thoughts are rarely the same as reality.

This tree I stumbled upon in early April of last year, and I too suspected nothing of its significance. I had been walking, and I lay down to sit and think beneath this tree, when looking up I saw something which astonished me. There, growing from its branch as an apple from an apple tree, was a brilliant sparkling white swan.

I jumped up when I saw it, as right above me, in the same fashion growing was the massive ferocious head of a great Grizzly bear.

I returned, slowly, to the base of the tree, and began to peer up at the mysterious animals hanging from this tree. There was a myriad of life there, raccoons and deer and birds and butterflies, and I suspect many other organisms as well, too small to see, or too peculiar for me to grasp their nature. They all grew from this ordinary and unceremonious tree in the forest.

As I watched, the white swan began to open her black pearly eyes and ruffle her elegant motherly feathers. All of a sudden, just as an apple may fall when it is ripe, this magnificent bird dropped headfirst to the ground with a tiny thump on the soft needles and moss. Curious still, and having compassion, I sauntered forward. Picking her up, I set her aright on her feet. She didn't look at me, as though she simply expected I would do this for her. Then, with a SCHWOOP SCHWOOP, she spread her wings and disappeared into the forest.

I have returned to this tree many times in my walks and each time I have watched it grow and helped those upside down animals on the ground. I still don't know who owns the tree, or from whence it came, but I have always been grateful for that day in the forest, with the tree and the Swan.

Dead Flat

I tell you, I see rocks every day. Matter o' fact, just so happens we' all livin' on a rock at this precise moment. A great big one at that. Sometimes I get to wonderein' why it is that we still lookin for rocks when we already got one, and everytime, it seems, when my mind comes 'round to that question, It gets a little sore again. You see, everybody wants more of the rock, no matter how much or how little they got to start with. But sooner or later, all that rock gonna land on top o' ya, gonna crush ya dead flat.

"Who's it gonna be this time?" The foreman cried out over the croud. "Two positions open, who wants to eat tonight?" I stepped a little closer, tryna' reach my hand a little higher. "You! Wallace." he said, pointing his two fingers at me with a grimace, like he knows I need it bad, but he don't really wanna take me on a third time in a row. Other fellas might get the picture, and they're liable to get upset ‘bout that. Got a lotta good men wantin’ to work, got only so many jobs. I twisted sideways and snaked my way out of the yellin’ crowd. A couple of the boys clapped my back, “Atta way, Wallace. Atta way.” They say.

So I shuffle on up to the box, Ol’ Pete takes two shovels, hands one to me, and we heads on down to the mine. Pete’s my workin’ buddy, He’s going strong for 55 and he’s ornery as all heck, but he’s got my back, and we get along, so all is fine and dandy. We head down to the mine, me and Pete, and we never looked back.

Grandma's Stairs

Manny walked across the room, passing Gramma just as he got to the stairs. They were dimly lit, but he knew the old dirty steps by heart, and he could always find Grandma by the shuffling of her feet. His bladder about to burst, Manny turned the corner onto the musky bottom landing. Just as he was about to dash up the steps, he felt an old, soft, arthritic hand grasp his forearm with the slow deliberateness of a three-toed sloth on Sunday morning.

A shiver coursed through his entire body. Her dusty old woman odor descended over his being and her delicate facial hairs glistened in the soft light. Manny turned to scream, "Grandma, I gotta pee!" But as he looked into her crafty ancient eyes, the guilty taste of a million fresh baked cookies held him in place.

Manny felt the house creak with that first step. “You better shuffle fast, Gramma,” he muttered under his breath.

“What was that, dearie?”

Fate is Blind

Cold, dead. Not seeing, not speaking, not moving, and best of all, not living. They said they were getting closer, but they have no idea. That detective, that stupendously foolish detective, always bumbling around the crime scenes, destroying all of my finely hidden clues. He'll never get any closer, never any warmer. The trail is getting cold before him, cold like death.

Soon she would be cold like death, but her fine delicate corpse was still warm for now. She seems so lifelike, though laying still now, as if she might only be stunned and in shock. But of course she isn't, and I know it because it was my heart which did the deed, just like all the others. My hand that held the waxy knife, and it was her doom which came to fruition tonight. And now for the fun to begin. A smile crosses my face, like an abandoned old woman might smile, hearing the dinner bell ring throughout her run down nursing home. And no one is there to see it. Bending down I breathe in deeply the soft aroma which lies over her. Her hair smells like oatmeal and daisies, her lips like softly caressed rose petals, and her hands smell like fear. I love the smell of fear on the cold lifeless hands of a victim. So close to life, but no longer in it.

I allowed the waxing knife to slide a little lower in my grip. I really should sharpen it, but a dull knife smooths the wax so much easier, and besides, someone might cut themselves on it. It all makes my work a little easier, so I let it go and adjust my grip. The cutting begins. She's soft like butter, muscles not yet stiff from rigor mortis. I carefully slide my knife in between vertebrae, a delicate process, and saw back and forth, periodically alternating angles as the blunt edge rakes through the nerves first one direction, then another. The warehouse air is frigid like the first day of winter, but she keeps me warm like a soft lover, and my hands relish in the soothing warmth flowing over and between them. Perhaps the deed had not been done as well as I had thought...but no matter. It's all done now.

Gently I caress her pallid cheeks, brushing away the tears and perhaps even leaving a thin smear of mascara behind, who can tell? I brush her oatmeal scented hair back and raise her up to inspect my work. Her face feels beautiful, even still, and I have a special place in mind for her.

Tomorrow they will come; they will look but not see truth. "How lifelike this one is!" they will exclaim, "The expression on this one so carefully crafted! That girl in the corner looks a bit fake don't you think? Her mascara is smeared too much. But no matter, these ones over here are the best!" And the foolish detectives will think nothing of it. I smile again. A blind detective, that's what they need. Appearances are all so deceptive. The feeling holds the truth. Only he could tell the warmth from cold, cold death.

When the Levee Breaks

Laid low against the ground, immersed in shallow mud, like a baby wrapped in blankets and peacefully dozing, was a rock. Flat like the heart monitor of a patient whose doctor is too late, the rock was perched amongst the silt and soil. The rock, not seeing and not hearing, was like a traumatized child, no longer caring for the outside world. A trickle of water came then, and a stream, and then the ditch filled with water, spilling over all about like a fat man in a petite restaurant booth, a roar like a terrible beast filled the air, and screams clogged by the spray followed in a crashing tumbling swirling blue black blanket. The rock saw none of this, heard none of this, knew none of this. Like a shadow in a dark world, the rock laid softly amongst the silt and soil.

A box in a box in a great big steel box, a radio held fast to its only familiar surroundings: As alone as a beached whale, or perhaps aloner. Black buttons and silver letters dotted it's face like stumps in a clear cut, but no one pressed them. No one was there to look at them. Wheels turn, but there is no pavement beneath them, only black tape. Only soft blues and hard rock is beneath the wheels, and they are stuck like a zeppelin made from lead. The radio flickered and, as if by the hand of God, or just liquefaction of the soils, life returned. A voice like a hot skillet thrust into a bucket of ice…"If it keeps on rainin', levee's gonna break...If it keeps on rainin' levee's gonna break…" For an empty stadium on the side of the road, the radio's voice wailed "When the levee breaks, I got no place to stay…"

Earthdance

A story with inspiration from the song "Earthdance" by Michael Sweeney

Snow's fallin. Gettin' cold out here, but I ain't shiverin'. That's nice. I look up, and I can see a great big swell of snowflakes, like a thousand head o' cattle in one big herd. Pilin' up all around like cotton in a strong wind, and rollin' off the ends of tree branches all around. Here I sit, admiring the beauty surrounding me. In the shelter of a great big fir tree I'm warm and covered up. The tree is magnificent, though surrounded by hundreds just like it, I sit there mesmerized. Bark splits into wide canyons and deep grooves, flowing with sap that seems lost in time. It occurs to me that ain't nobody's ever touched this tree before. So peaceful and pristine was the scene that I just sit, alone in the forest, drawing in the sweet, clear, crisp cold mountain air. I ain't moving a bit, leaned softly against the bark, sensing the scent of falling snow and rough fir needles, until finally my eyes fall softly shut like a pair of boring bluish-grey books at the end of a long study session. The snow continues to pile around me.

"We're ready for you Mr Todd." The peppy young british voice reverberated through lobby. Her neatly pressed slacks were an awful rusty brown, unfortunately the least distracting thing she'd worn all week. Despite looking better in a starched white lab coat than any of her daily clothes, Lauren was a good intern, pretty, and always mentally prepared for the tasks ahead of her. Maybe I'll ask her to dinner after the tests, I thought. With awkward scenarios running nervously through my head, we walked through the steel doors and down the long highway to the test room.

"These kryo-whatsamajigs… " I said to Lauren. "They worked on the chimps, right?" I gave her a cheap grin to let her know I was joking. Her gaze was dead serious as she replied,

"Our animal tests have had greater than 93% success rates throughout almost all contemporary data sets."

Jesus. I thought. What a cold-case. "And, uh, the 7%? What happened to them?" I looked at her, and her eyes, like beautiful grey windows to her frozen soul, gaped back.

"Our window of opportunity is drawing nearer, Mr. Todd. We must keep our eyes on the prize. And the prize... is kryo-sleep." She pushed open the cold black windowless doors, and the dampness of my fear evaporated with wonder.

"These...uh...I'm gonna go in one o' these?" She nodded tersely, but my mind was hardly with her anymore.

"Shall I begin the preliminary physical tests?"

"Go for it." I said. "What's the worst that could happen?"

Stepping out of the whispering maze of neck high grass, I see the sight my eyes have been searching for. It's the most beautiful sight I've ever seen, getting better each time I see it. My toes sink a little deeper into that sun warmed sand and feel the tropical gulf breeze blowin' my hair back and filling my lungs with the scent of sardines, salt, and surfers. Man alive, have I missed this place. I fall into a full on sprint as the waves of excitement meld with the warm waves of the gulf shore. Most beautiful land on earth, don't let anyone tell ya different. Boy have I missed these waves.

"I had a really nice time last night." She said softly, her eyes subtly hinting what might happen to her if her boss found out. Dr. Felitz was a kind eyed man, but his tolerance for relationships in the workplace seemed uncharacteristically low, I supposed there was some personal story about that that I just didn't know. "Thank you." Maybe those eyes didn't lead to such a frozen soul after all.

"Maybe next time we can stay in, make a little dinner ourselves." She nodded, perhaps a little too vigorously, but it was alright. Eagerness was a good look on her. My eyes followed her as she started to walk away and turned back to face me.

"There's other news as well, if you'll care to hear it." She continued in her usual overtly professional way. "The results of human testing have been conclusive. They tell me that you may be one of only 4 people in the world who can survive such a long deep sleep period as is required to make the trip." Her face suddenly downcast, as if to conceal her disappointment in what she had to say. "Your shuttle will launch at 0800 Wednesday next. You will report at 0430 for final briefing." With the finality of a cursed doctor in a cancer ward, she remarked, "You will be the first man on the ice planet."

I push through the reeds and smell the muddy air, wafting warm microbial life into my nostrils. I take one, two and then three steps down, my feet sinking a little into the silty bank. The gnats are gettin' all agitated in my face, and I eat a few on accident, but they aren't anywhere near what's on my mind right now. This must be the last untouched fishin' hole in all of south Texas, and I'm the guy that finds it. Man I can just hear them bass sittin' right in the shade o' that log and singin', naturally, in their bass clef voices, about the sun gettin' hotter and the cool of the water. I set out my tackle, sittin' down to tie on a new lure, and I cock my rod back just a bit, lookin' to cast out right behind that stump over there. Slow back and quick forward just like the twang of a bow-string. I let the lure fly in a gorgeous arc to end in a soft ker-plunk and...

crackle...crackle...Mr. Todd, do you copy?...crackle...James, talk to us. How do you feel?...crackle.

"Whaa... ?" Is all I can manage to croak in reply. "I...I...am.... .fine. Wha?" My entire body tingles numb like a great big shot o' novocaine, and my eyes feel like they been glued shut for years.

crackle...Good. You're awake...crackle...You've been asleep for quite a while Mr. Todd...crackle...crackle...how is Pluto these days, son?...

"Plu...ah, oh. Yes sir. Wednesday next sir. 0430 sir," I stammered. "I'll be there, sir."

crackle...crackle..Son, the Wednesday next to which you...crackle...are referring happened almost exactly 12 and one half years ago. You've already been...crackle...to the ice planet, son, and as you may recall, you sent us some mighty fine scientific data back here in Houston....crackle...

He's talkin' a little too quick for me to understand now, and I just let my mind go blank for a few precious moments. It feels a little too claustrophobic in this...hold on just a minute...where the hell am I? I look down, and see only blackness from my chest down. Looking up, I see only blackness. There's a tiny orange light next to me, but I can't turn my head to face it. I can see what look like little pinpricks of light just ahead of me...but those...those can't be...stars? I don't remember being...and they sure do sparkle...but I'm in...but there's no way...12 and one half years?!?! Jimminy Christmas! Where the hell...what the...when did I...? The disembodied voice returned in my ear.

It's alright, son. We'll get you squared away as soon as you get your feet back on solid ground, eh?...crackle...we woke you up for something that may be very special to you...crackle...landing sequence begins in 4 minutes and 27 seconds...crackle The pinpricks began to shift in my vision. Son, say hello to Earth...crackle...it's been a long time.

The pinpricks have moved out of my vision, and my little visual world is devoured by the glory of Mother Earth. Glowing golden in hues of brown, green, white and blue, she shimmers like surface of a big ol' lake just at sundown. Memories, images, thoughts, flashbacks, so much information floods into my mental canals. A wave of molten emotion pours over me like syrup over Sunday mornin' flapjacks. I don't even know how long it's been, but man alive have I missed my home. Like a dream, suddenly I can remember vague images of a hard landing on a dark and desolate night out in space. For a moment, my eyes close and I see...blue...clouds under my feet. I step...I fly...I fall... I land with a great crack...sinking knee deep. The sensors...the computer...radio...robot...doors closing... eyes closing...senses fading...

Snow's fallin. Gettin' cold out here, but I ain't shiverin'. That's nice. I look up, and I can see a great big swell of snowflakes, like a thousand head o' cattle in one big...

crackle...son, we're picking up on error messages sent by your Kryo-induced REM stasis unit... crackle...we believe you may need to do some repair work...crackle...need to move quickly, you have 2 minutes and 48 seconds before re-entry, and we have no idea how these...crackle...may affect your ability to surv...crackle...crackle...crackle...auxiliar y pack and remove the panel. Can you do that?

"Uh...I...could you repeat the last part of tha..." ...unfortunately the least distracting thing she'd worn all week. Despite looking better in a starched white lab coat than any of her daily clothes...

Mr. Todd, I'm going to need you to respond...crackle...1 minute and...crackle...much time remaining...crackle...

I'm vaguely aware of my eyes flickering open and shut at a rapid rate, but I know I need to fix it, whatever this voice is talking about. "This must be the last untouched fishin' hole in all of south Texas." I reply, my hands suddenly springing to action of their own accord. I press the orange button, and a little panel folds down. Wires and tubes riddle the carbon-fiber surface. Without instruction, my hands seem to know each component of the hardwire panel, testing and tugging each component until I find the faulty one.

crackle...Mr. Todd you have 21 seconds remaining. I need to you to listen to me...crackle...You are not in Texas, you are in outer space...crackle...

I pressed the panel back into the dark surface firmly, but not too forcefully, and held the orange button for three blinks.

"Maybe next time we can stay in, make a little dinner ourselves." I said, hoping to calm the disembodied voice from Houston.

You have less than 10 seconds...8,7,6...crackle...4,3,2...wait...crackle... son, you've done it! You are back online!

An audible sigh of relief came through the crackling feedback. "Hey, do me a favor...call up the research center, have 'em put Lauren Dawson on the line. The intern, Lauren Dawson." I say confidently, the fuzzy details of my life starting to pull together. "I'm gonna ask her to marry me." A silence follows.

crackle...Ah, son...The Human Kryo Testing department has never taken on any interns... we're not sure what to say...crackle

"But...we said we would wait for each other... she"

crackle...preparing landing sequence in T-10 seconds...crackle...

I let the lure fly in a gorgeous arc to end in a soft ker-plunk. As it sinks, I jig on it a little, just reelin' in a tiny bit, I can feel those bass just sniffin' that bad boy. "Man, that smell good." say one bass.

"You want it?" say the other.

"Go for it, bubba. What's the worst that could happen?"

Obboney

Judith Caroline Jones is 2 years old. That is to say, she would be 2 years old if she were like other kids. If she were like her older sister, she would still be stumbling around in their parents' small flat in Queens. Judith isn't like other kids, though, and today she is 13 Jude-years old.

The kitten in her arms was a gift on Jude's very first birthday, when she was one, but only looked four or five. His name is Captain Shadow William Nemo, or Nemo for short. Jud loves him with all her heart because he is all she has and knows in the world. The doctors said that her body would age quickly, but they couldn't say just how her intellect might develop. That was a long time ago. A real long time ago, in fact, 3 jude-years ago.

Jude doesn't live with her parents in New Yorek anymore, not with the Doctors and nurses in Washington. Jude lives in big wet Oregon, in Obboney Oregon, and she lives there with Nemo and she learns something new every day.

Today she learned that no one opens the towel closets at motels because the towels are all on the counters. Tonight she will learn that towel closets are too small to sleep in. Last night she learned that outside is too cold. Jude wants to go home, but she doesn't have a home anymore. She only has the towels, Obbony, and Nemo. Jude is getting hungry.

They Say His Name is “Moccasins”

It was cold the next morning, when I woke up. It’s always cold on the mountain, but this morning it was a different kind of cold you don’t just feel in your bones. You can hear it in the silence that rings like a bell all around you. You can taste it, like when you burn the hell out of your tongue on some coffee, and just for a moment you can taste the pain. It was painfully cold on that morning when I woke up.

I pulled my hat low over my ears and took my blanket with me as I slid my body out the tent flap and into the camp, careful not to wake any of the other guys. As I rolled over and maneuvered my way up to standing in the snow there, I surveyed the scene. Our guide was already up, wearing nothing but a wife-beater and basketball shorts under his parka. A beast of a man, though standing only five-ten or so, maybe a little more, he must have weighed a hundred and ninety pounds. He wore his curly hair short and his beard long and black, he had a tattoo of a fox chasing a rabbit on his left hand, and they say his name was "Moccasins."

Now, it's difficult for me to say much about Moccasins, this being my first climb and all. I knew he was in his mid-thirties and from somewhere in the US. I knew he used to do some kind of pro fighting or something, and when I asked one of the other guides why "moccasins," he said, "he's walked a mile in just about everybody's moccasins, and now that he's walked all that way, his feet sure are sore." Turns out, nobody really knew much about him; he didn't talk much, but he had these blue eyes, the most piercing you've ever seen, and I was pretty sure he could size up a man's whole life just by looking at him with those eyes.

So it was just me and Moccasins on that painfully cold morning at Camp 3 way up on that mountain. I waddled, as bundled as I was, towards the fire and sat down on a sling chair. The warmth of the flames made my feet grateful as I stretched them out in that little thawed area around the pit. Moccasins didn't look at me as I approached, but he gestured toward the kettle hanging over the flaming logs. I graciously poured myself some coffee, which was the most relieving thing I'd done in days, and sat there next to that fire with Moccasins, watching the sunrise. I didn't look at him and he didn't look at me. Truth be told, I was more concerned with the distinct lack of goose bumps on his exposed ink-covered calves, despite it being well below -15° F out there.

After about ten minutes of this, Moccasins spoke. He didn't look at me, didn't even turn his head, just looked straight into the rising sun, bringing the first rays of the new day. "Where you come from, Chris?" he asked.

Caught completely off guard, my mind floundered for a couple of seconds. "Uh...Illinois." I managed to blurt out. I looked shiftily at him, to see if his countenance had changed, but he remained passive. Just staring into the sun.

“Is that right. North or South?”

“What?”

“You come outta the top end o’ Illinois, or the bottom?”

“Yeah, uh… top…I guess.” I said, kicking myself for stuttering so much. Unsure of how to handle this encounter with a man I hadn’t even known could speak, I just continued like I would with any other mortal. “You?”

“Iowa. Yessir, Davenport, Iowa. Born and bred.”

I started to reply in a manner befitting morning conversations with strangers, but he just kept talking, never looking at me, always just looking into the sun. I said, “So is northern or south… ”

“Do you know I haven’t been back there in 6 years? That’s a Goddamned long time.”

To this I had no response, so I just let it continue, occasionally glancing down at the goosebumpless legs.

"My father…my father. Fuck." he said, his eyes starting to water from staring into the sun so long. I looked on in complete astonishment as this human wall of stone continued to speak. "I was 10 years old, backseat, brand new BMW, top down. It was his baby. Ross, he was in the front seat, he's my kid brother. Funny thing about that day, had a sunrise looked just like this one, how the fuck we even know we don't die today? This might be it for guys like you and me."

Moccasins looked at me for the first time, and I realized that the tears in his eyes weren't from looking into the sun. I was frozen, I could say nothing, but it didn't matter, because he wasn't finished. "Me and Ross, just bickerin' like always, we was fightin' over the radio or something. Dad, he looks at me and Ross, an' he gets this smile, see."

Puffing up to the size that all boys perceive the figure of their fathers to be, Moccasins began his expressive imitation of his father's speech. "'Boys, fighting isn't the answer. You've got to choose your battles--sometimes it's best to just let it go.'" He said, the squeaky voice that he did so instinctively seemed alien coming from his bearded face. The sarcastic look faded from his face and he deflated a bit as he continued.

"But me and Ross, couple o' Zippos, we didn't even hear it, just kept going for that knob." He paused for a moment, brushing the new ice crystals off his cheek, and then continued. "All the sudden, we both hit the seat backs hard, and dad's hands are off the wheel, and -- and we're spinning and there's glass everywhere, an' smoke an' shit. All I see is Rossy halfway through the windshield, and Dad, he's sitting wit' his head down, all calm like he's worried tire pressure might be low or somethin'."

Moccasins had ice in his beard now, and a couple other guys were starting to poke their heads out of the tents, but he focused on me. I could feel his eyes cutting into me, gauging reaction like a boxer's jab cuts through his opponent's guard and gauges range. I was starting to regain my senses at this point, but could not fathom what great section of the blue this was coming out of.

"They said somebody drunk, drivin' some kinda semi truck. Came blowin' through the red light and Dad, he just can't stop, he just swerves off, but it's the wrong way, and Ross's side hits 'em full on. Now Ross, he's sittin' there, all kinds of bloody, and glass everywhere, and Dad he's sittin' there, just lookin' at the fuckin' tire gauge. They got the guy, and took him to court, and Dad says he don't even wanna press charges. And that was the day my life started. I was so scared I couldn' even move, and the doctor said I got depression. I just kept thinkin' about it, and the more I thought, the more I come to realize. Dad got so scared when he saw that truck, see, he couldn't do nothin' about it. And after that he's so scared, he won't even press charges, he says. I never forgave him for that, maybe I shoulda'. I promised myself that day that nothing would ever scare me so bad that I couldn't do nothin' about it. I found out that fear wants to be your master, but you gotta be the master of your fears. And it's funny. That day had a sunrise just like today"

I hung on every word, as did everyone in the camp, and we all waited, hoping for something more from this beast of a man, whose words prior to this we could have counted on one hand, to say a little bit more. He didn't. After a bit, he abruptly stood, causing us all to jump back. Goosebumps starting to form on his taught calf muscles, he exclaimed, "It's fucking cold out here!" and stormed into his tent. I've heard not another word from Moccasins since.

ABOUT THE AUTHOR

John McGee is a Senior, class of 2014, at Philomath High School. A writer since he was just a whippersnapper, John enjoys writing poetry and music, and never misses a chance to tell a good story. Enrolled in a creative writing class, he was faced with the opportunity to compile his writing works into a definitive collection, his first published book, *Free Spirit: Face Cloud*. After high school, John plans to attend Oregon State University for a four year degree in mechanical engineering, and maybe, you know, play a little music, chill. Stuff like that. In the meantime, enjoy his writing herein, and check out his new album, "Eulogy" on SoundCloud at JohnMcGee7

Peace and Love, everybody!

www.ingramcontent.com/pod-product-compliance
Ingram Content Group UK Ltd.
Pitfield, Milton Keynes, MK11 3LW, UK
UKHW020216250726
13967UKWH00001B/36

9 781312 058606